·LA TURISTA·

LA TURISTA

A Play in Two Acts

BY SAM SHEPARD

The Bobbs-Merrill Company, Inc.
Indianapolis • New York

The Bobbs-Merrill Company, Inc.
A Subsidiary of Howard W. Sams & Co., Inc.,
Publishers / Indianapolis • Kansas City • New York

Editor's note: LA TURISTA opened at The American Place Theater in New York City on March 4, 1967, for a limited engagement of two weeks. It was directed by Jacques Levy, and the cast for the original production were as follows:

SALEM	JOYCE AARON
KENT	SAM WATERSTON
BOY	LAWRENCE BLOCK
DOCTOR	MICHAEL LOMBARD
SON	JOEL NOVACK
DOC	MICHAEL LOMBARD
SONNY	LAWRENCE BLOCK

•FOR JOYCE•

•INTRODUCTION•

A few lines, as a prologue to my review of Sam Shepard's *La Turista* which is reprinted here just as it was written immediately after seeing the play. I have, in the months since, thought again and again about this play and the imaginative strength of it. From the moment I entered the American Place Theater I was caught up in the violent energy of a new work. It is hard to forget the bright, bright yellow and orange set, so hard and brilliant, so open, glaring and aggressive, that announced the bright, glaring, aggressive brilliance of the play.

Some further thoughts about the text occur to me. Nothing is harder to come by than a truly meaningful central image, one that opens out to possibility, encourages invention. For some reason we must, aesthetically, be satisfied with the image, or situation, on the first plane of concreteness. Without that it is hard to give assent to the elaborations that will follow; in a sense, you have to enter the structure the author gives you before you are willing to see what is inside. In this play the identity of the person—the tourist—and his affliction, that humbling diarrhea—"la turista"—are signified by a single word. This word and the two things it represents are the bare center of the play, the ruling image. The sickness is a sort of a joke—that kills.

Salem and Kent are literally tourists in Mexico in the first act. In the second, which in point of time takes place before the

first, Kent is on another kind of journey—I won't say "trip"—
in which American rhetoric is offered for his cure just as the
blood of freshly killed chickens had been offered in "primitive" Mexico. Neither works.

Perhaps the characters are not profitably thought of as characters at all, They are actors, parodists. They slip from style
to style; they carry a few props around with them as they
change their roles; they "freeze" when they want to withdraw
from the action on the stage. The essence of their being is
energy, verbal energy. In the restless inventiveness of their
parodies and tirades, a storm of feeling and experience blows
across the stage. The parts are arias. In the last section of
Act II Doc and Kent "sing" an extraordinary duet. These arias
have to do with death. It is amazing the number of "deaths"
that will fit the text: Vietnam, Santo Domingo, racial violence,
drop-outs, colonialism.

When I wrote about the play, I gave more attention to the
critics than I think it is worth now. And yet that was a part of
the scenery in which the first production of the play took
place. I would have felt very sorry if I had missed seeing it
and I must confess that I hated to see it close. But this play
lives on the page, and that is a rare thing nowadays.

September, 1967

March, 1967

La Turista by Sam Shepard, in a dazzling production at the
American Place Theater, is a work of superlative interest. The
reviewers have not been invited to submit an evaluation of the
play. It is merely there, for a month, appearing for the mem-
bership of the American Place and for those who find their
way to it. I have no knowledge of the intentions and feelings

about the reviewers of those responsible for this play; I went to it of my own free will and write about it under no duress and without asking permission. Still, it appears logical that when a play invites the press it is making a sort of plea or demand that the reviewer, under his contractual obligations to his publication, offer some comment about what he has seen. He may not have wished to go and he may not wish to write; he is a captive, arbitrarily condemned to the formation of an opinion. The production, by its foolhardy solicitations, condemns itself to the recognition of the opinions. Play and critic, thereby, become linked like suspect and detective.

The night I saw *La Turista* the American Place audience was, for the most part, utterly depressing; middle-aged, middle class, and rather aggressively indifferent: a dead weight of alligators, dozing and grunting before muddily sliding away. It felt like nothing so much as those same old evenings in our theater, evenings with the reviewers spaced about like stop signs. A further step in the liberation of the theater became evident: not only must the reviewers be freed of their obligation to go to a play, but the audience they have created, their bent twigs, should not be the object of special encouragement. It is hard to imagine anyone acting under the influence of the inchoate homilies of, for instance, Richard Watts who looks after our local and national morals for us, but, even in the case of *La Turista,* one could *imagine* a line slowly forming outside some box office and the people whispering, "Walter Kerr sort of liked it a little, and you know *he* never likes anything." But, indeed, what good does it do a man to go to see something he won't like just because the reviewers have told him to do so? He would be better off at home. Our new American theater cannot play to the old audience; it must have a new one.

In *La Turista* there is the poignant meeting on some pure level of understanding of playwright, director, and actor: the sort of unity that makes the Royal Shakespeare's production of *The Homecoming* so rare. Jacques Levy, the director, is a theatrical talent of unremitting inspiration. The actors are all first-rate, but in Sam Waterston the play has a young actor of such versatility and charm that one hardly knows how to express the degree of his talents. With this play, the promise of the lofts of off-off Broadway, the dedication and independence, come to the most extraordinary fulfillment. You do not feel you are being given a package, assembled for a purpose, and in some ways this is disconcerting to the senses. The audience, accustomed to ensembles created as a calculation, may feel left out, slow to respond, trapped by a sluggish metabolism. In the long run, what is so beautiful is the graceful—in spite of the frenzied energy—concentration of the work as a whole, and for that, if one would take it in, the audience also has to work.

Sam Shepard, the author of *La Turista,* is twenty-three years old and even so he is not new to the theater. He is not being "discovered" in this production. His plays have been off-off, in the Café La Mama repertory; he has been at the Cherry Lane and will soon be in print. *La Turista* is his most ambitious play thus far but still it is in the same style and voice as *Chicago* and his other one-act plays. The scene opens on an electrifying set: a bright, bright formica yellow hotel room in Mexico. A young American couple—Salem and Kent—are sitting up in their twin beds. They are covered with a deep bronze suntan make-up and are holding their arms out stiffly. On the beach, as a part of their vacation, they have gotten a painful sunburn. They talk of first, second, and third—and *fourth* degree burns.

> "Well, the epidermis is actually cooked, fried like a piece of meat over a charcoal fire. The molecular structure of the fatty tissue is partially destroyed by the sun rays and so the blood rushes to the surface to repair the damage."
>
> ". . . It's just the blood rushing to the surface."

Mock scientific dialogue, inserted merely for itself, delivered in a cool, matter-of-fact way, but sharply, insistently, is characteristic of the writing. (Of course, the couple with their expensive, painful sunburns will bring to mind those other burns of our time.) The players hardly ever look at each other. There is a feeling of declamation, rather than of conversation or dialogue. And yet the monologues do not at all suggest that banality of Broadway—the "failure of communication"— but actually are quite the opposite. They are an extreme of communication. Kent, the young man, also has, in addition to his sunburn, "la turista," the intestinal distress that affects Americans when they visit poor countries like Mexico. At this point in the play, a young Mexican enters. He is one of the world's poor, with his American phrases ("I had to follow that cat around with a palm fan while he scored on all the native chicks.")—he begs and yet he is intractable, unmanageable. He spits in the young American's face.

As the act progresses, Kent becomes very ill. Two wonderfully absurd witch doctors, Mexican style, are brought in, with live roosters, candles, voodoo and crucifixes. Kent dies, a sacrifice to "la turista"—his lack of resistance to the germs of the country he arrogantly patronizes with his presence. The second act has all the same elements as the first, but they are acted out in a Summit Hotel sort of room in America and the witch doctors are two circuit rider charlatans in Civil War dress. Here Kent dies of sleeping sickness, or perhaps he is on drugs; in any case he has an American disease this time—he doesn't like to be awake. His final monologue is a psychedelic tirade—and he jumps, in his pajamas, through the hotel wall, leaving the print of the outlines of his body in the wallpaper.

George Eliot said that she wrote her novels out of the belief in "the orderly sequence by which the seed brings forth a crop of its kind." We all have a nostalgia and longing for this order because it has been the heart of European fiction and drama. Incident after incident, each growing out of the other, united in a chain of significant motivation, of cause and effect —moments of human destiny strung out like beads on a string. This is what we mean, perhaps, when we say we "understand" a work of literary art. Yet each decade brings us the conviction that this order is no longer present to the serious writer. It is most appealing to those writers who construct their works for some possibility of the marketplace. The episodic, the obscurely related, the collection of images, moods: connections in fiction and also in drama have become like those of poetry. Tone and style hold the work together, create whatever emotional effect it will have upon us. Out of episodes and images, characters and conflicts are made, but they are of a blurred and complex sort.

Formless images and meaningless happenings are peculiarly oppressive to the spirit, and the inanities of the experimental theater could make a man commit suicide. Sam Shepard, on the other hand, possesses the most impressive literary talent and dramatic inventiveness. He is voluble, in love with long, passionate, intense monologues (both of the acts end in these spasms of speech) which almost petrify the audience. His play ends with sweating, breathless actors in a state of exhaustion. The characters put on a shawl and begin to declaim like an auctioneer at a slave mart, or a cowboy suit and fall into Texas harangues. They stop in the midst of jokes, for set pieces, some fixed action from childhood, perhaps influenced by the bit in Albee's *Zoo Story*. Despair and humor, each of a peculiarly expressive kind, are the elements out of which the script of the play is made. The effect is very powerful and if it cannot be reduced to one or two themes it is still clearly about us and our lives. The diction, the acting, the direction, the ideas are completely American and it is our despair and humor Shepard gets onto the stage.

To return to the decision about the critics: it is a sacrificial act of the most serious sort. It means nothing less than, after a fixed short run, if one is lucky enough to have that, the play may suffer simple cessation for want of those and good and bad advertisements combed from the newspapers and television. Perhaps it is only young people, free of deforming ambitions, who would have the courage to submit to such a test. Or perhaps it is the strength of their art that allows them to wait for what will come or not come. There are worse things than silence.

Elizabeth Hardwick

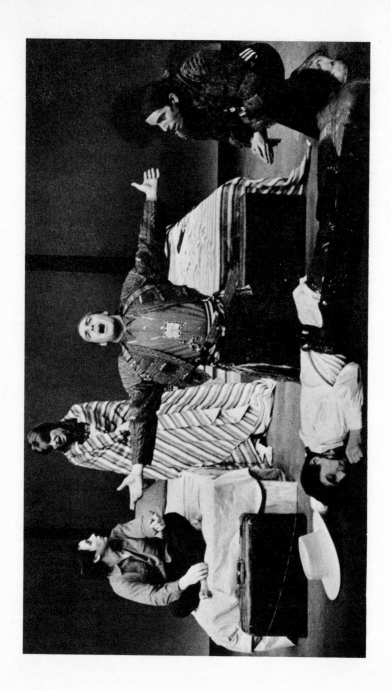

LA TURISTA
ACT ONE

SCENE

Two single beds with clean white sheets and pillows upstage center. Between the beds is a small yellow desk with a telephone on it. The entire upstage wall is bright canary yellow. A bright orange door in the wall to stage right with the words "CUARTO DE BANO" printed on it in red letters. Another bright orange door, stage left, with a cardboard sign hanging by string from the doorknob. The sign reads: "NO MOLE-STAR POR FAVOR" in red letters. At the foot of each bed, on the floor, are two huge over-stuffed suitcases. A large fan hangs from the ceiling, center stage. Salem, a woman in pan-ties and bra, sits on the stage left bed propped up with a pillow, facing the audience and reading Life magazine. Kent, a man in underwear, sits in the same position on the stage right bed reading Time magazine. Both Salem and Kent have bright red skin. The lights come up to bright yellow, the fan is on, Salem *and* Kent *sit reading for a while. They continue reading as they talk.*

SALEM/ The woman in—where was it? Puerto Juarez or something. The very rich Spanish woman. Remember? The young woman with her mother who spoke such good English. Very rich.

KENT/ What did she say?

SALEM/ She said the white of an egg is what you use for second or third degree burns. The pain is eased right away. What happens when the skin is burned? I mean what actually happens?

KENT/ Well, the epidermis is actually cooked, fried like a piece of meat over a charcoal fire. The molecular structure of the fatty tissue is partially destroyed by the sun rays, and so the blood rushes to the surface to repair the damage.

SALEM/ So your skin doesn't really turn red like magic, it's just the blood rushing to the surface.

KENT/ Right.

SALEM/ So Mexicans aren't really tan, are they. They just have darker skin, tougher skin with a tighter fatty molecular structure.

KENT/ I think that's an anthropological argument now, where some say the dark skinned people of the earth were born that way to begin with for camouflage reasons to protect them against death, and others say it was to protect them against the sun.

SALEM/ It doesn't make much difference.

KENT/ No. But the sun theory seems to make more sense. Well no, I guess the death theory makes more sense since Islandic people, people who live in snowy places, have light skin to match the snow. So I guess it has to do with camouflage, since camouflage has to do with deceiving death.

SALEM/ What about Eskimos.

KENT/ Eskimos are more on the yellow side, aren't they. More Mongoloid. Eskimos aren't really dark.

SALEM/ Well, Mexicans are more Mongoloid than Negroid and you call them dark.

KENT/ That's true. (Kent *jumps to his feet and starts for the stage right door and then stops short.*)

SALEM/ Que paso!

KENT/ I started to feel it coming and then it stopped. I don't know whether it's coming or stopping.

SALEM/ Que turista! No!

KENT/ Speak English, will you. (*He starts again for the door and stops.*)

SALEM/ Is it dysentery?

KENT/ I don't know. It starts and stops.

SALEM/ (*Like a nurse*) Cramps in the stomach?

KENT/ Slight ones.

SALEM/ Nausea?

KENT/ Slight.

SALEM/ Rumbling in the bowels?

KENT/ A little.

SALEM/ Esta turista? (Kent *starts to run for the door and stops again.*)

KENT/ You sound glad or something.

SALEM/ No. Yo es muy simpatico.

KENT/ We both ate the same food, you know, so you'll be getting it soon too.

SALEM/ My metabolism is very high.
(Kent *returns to the stage right bed, picks up the magazine, and continues to read.*)

KENT/ Relaxation is the thing you seek. You spend thousands of hours and dollars and plane rides to get to a place for relaxation. To just disappear for a while. And you wind up like this. With diarrhea.

SALEM/ You came here to disappear?

KENT/ That's right. Didn't you? To relax and disappear.

SALEM/ What would you do if you did disappear?

KENT/ Nothing. I'd be gone.

SALEM/ I ask you that face to face. It deserves to be answered.

KENT/ Do you know how soon it is before you can start peeling it?

SALEM/ Not before it's dead, I can tell you that much. Right now it stings. That means it's alive and hurting. Pretty soon it itches. Then you know it's dying. Then it stops itching and you know it's dead. Then you can start peeling. Not before.

KENT/ You can start peeling as soon as it begins to itch. I know that much. That's when you itch so you scratch it and that gets you peeling.

SALEM/ You can't start before the itching stops.

KENT/ Why not? You could even start while it's still stinging if you wanted. You could even start before it starts stinging and get a head start.

SALEM/ And then really get burned. You'd be in sad shape then, boy.

KENT/ Then you start peeling again.

SALEM/ There's only three layers, you know. It doesn't go on forever.

KENT/ Obviously you've never heard of the fourth degree burn. A fourth degree burn is unheard of because it's never happened, but one day it will, and doctors will be dismayed from coast to coast, and a new word will be born into their language. *The Fourth Degree Burn!*

SALEM/ What is it like! What is it like!
(Kent *rises on his bed and demonstrates for her.*)

KENT/ The fourth degree burn comes about after the most extreme and excruciating process has taken its course. The first degree has already occurred and a layer has dropped away almost of its own accord. Effortlessly it floats to the floor at your feet and piles around your ankles like sheets of Kleenex. The second degree comes with a little more shock and a little more pain. It scrapes off like dust and covers the sheets.

SALEM/ And now for the third!

KENT/ Yes! But the third takes time. The third begins slowly and creeps along the surface, grabbing hold and easing up. Biting down and relaxing away until the spaces get fewer and the biting gets harder. Everything burns and everything you touch is as hot as the sun. You stand away from everything else. You stand in mid-air with space all around you. The ground is on fire. The breeze feels like boiling-hot water. The moon is just like the sun. You become a flame and dance in mid-air. The bottom is blue. The middle is yellow and changes to green. The top is red and changes to orange. The breeze dances with you. The flame reaches up and then shrinks and bursts into sparks. The ground bursts into flame and circles the breeze. The sparks dart through the breeze and dash back and forth hitting up against the flames, and——
(*The stage left door opens, and a dark skinned boy, but not Negro, enters with bare feet and carrying a shoe shine kit. Both* Salem *and* Kent *scream and pull the top sheet of their beds over their bodies so just their heads are sticking out. The boy crosses in between the beds and just stares at them with his hand out.*)

Basta!

SALEM/ Vaya!

KENT/ Give him some money.

SALEM/ How do you say go away?

KENT/ Just give him some money.

SALEM/ I can't, it's in the suitcase.

KENT/ Well get it.

SALEM/ How do I get it?

KENT/ Crawl down under the sheet and get it.

SALEM/ Can't you get up?

KENT/ Salem, you're the closest one to the money.

SALEM/ Oh, all right.
(*She crawls underneath the sheet to the foot of the bed and sticks her hand out to reach the suitcase on the floor. As she does this,* Kent *speaks to the* Boy, *who just stares with his hand out.*)

KENT/ She'll have it for you in just a second.

BOY/ Lustre?

KENT/ She'll be right with you. If you weren't so poor, I'd kick you out on your ass.

BOY/ Lustre?

KENT/ Just hold on. Are they taught by their mothers and fathers to look more despondent than they really are?

(Salem *is still under the sheet and struggling to open the suitcase.*)

SALEM/ Sometimes.

KENT/ It works. All they have to do is stare. A blank stare does more than a grimace.

SALEM/ Just stare back.

KENT/ If I was that poor I'd kill myself. I wouldn't pretend I was sadder than I really was. I couldn't take it all the time, everywhere I went, every time I got up, knowing I was no better off and no worse than yesterday. Just the same all the time. Just poor.

BOY/ Lustre?

KENT/ To just go on and on, getting older and older, and staying just as poor, and maybe even getting poorer. And pretending all the time I was poorer than I was.

SALEM/ That's why the mothers sometimes give their babies away to tourists, because they know there's a better chance of them getting rich.

KENT/ Who'd want a poor kid?

SALEM/ Some people who can't have a rich one.

BOY/ Lustre?

KENT/ What's he want?

SALEM/ To shine your shoes.

KENT/ No shine. Go away. Basta!

BOY/ Lustre?

KENT/ No! (*He puts his head under the sheet. The* Boy *just stands.*)

SALEM/ Let him shine your shoes.

KENT/ No! I can't even look at him. His hands are full of pork grease; his eyes are red; his breath smells. Get him away.

SALEM/ Ah ha!
(*She opens the suitcase, and money pours out of it. She gestures with her hand for the* Boy *to come and take some money. Her hand is the only visible part of her.*)

SALEM/ Aqui niño! Aqui! (*The* Boy *keeps staring at* Kent, *who remains under the sheet.*)

KENT/ Is he gone?

SALEM/ Chico. Aqui. Quiere diñero? Por favor. Aqui.

KENT/ What's he doing?

SALEM/ Will you be quiet. He won't even move. He doesn't even know there's free money to be had.

KENT/ Great.

SALEM/ Niño por favor. Aqui. Es muy bueno.
(*This speech should sound like an English safari hunter warning somebody about a man-eating lion. During this,* Salem's *hand can be seen waving money at the* Boy. Kent *stays under the sheet through the speech.*)

KENT/ He'll never leave now. He's probably never seen a house like this in his life. He grew up in a village, in a hut. He nursed his mother's milk until he was four and a half and then almost died from dysentery at the time he was weaned. He's eaten nothing but rice and beans all his life and slept on the dirt and sold dirty Coca Cola to passing cars. He'll never leave now no matter how much you give him. The fan to him is like the finest air conditioning. The beds to him are like two Rolls Royces. He likes the sound of my voice because it's so strange and soothing and he knows I'm talking about him, and he likes that because, where he lives in the jungle, nobody talks about him, because he's nothing different to them. They're all the same and silent, and sleep and walk around each other like herds of wild boar getting ready to run or kill each other, depending upon the air and the wind and the sun.

SALEM/ Well what shall we do about that.

KENT/ Can you reach the phone?

SALEM/ You're closer to it than me.

KENT/ O.K. Maybe the manager will know what to do. (Kent *starts to reach for the phone. The Boy rushes to the phone and pulls it out of the wall, then crosses downstage center with it and sets it on the floor. He sits down next to the phone and sets the shoe shine kit down and smiles at the audience. Throughout the following, the Boy makes different monster faces at the audience, from sticking his tongue out to giving them the finger.*)

SALEM/   (*Still under the sheet*) What happened?

KENT/   (*Now visible*) The little prick pulled the phone out of the wall. (Salem *laughs*.) All right!
(Kent *jumps out of bed and crosses down to the* Boy, *who just sits center stage facing the audience.*)

SALEM/   (*Still under the sheets*) Are you out of bed, dear?

KENT/   (*To the* Boy) You have to leave now. This is not your home. Go back from where you come from.
(*The* Boy *stands and spits in* Kent's *face. Kent rushes back to the bed and wipes the spit off with the sheet. The* Boy *sits again and continues making faces to the audience.*)

KENT/   OOOoooh! Oh my God! Aaaah! Spit! He spit on me! Oh no! Oh my God! Jesus! He spit on me!

SALEM/   What's the matter?

KENT/   He spit! He spit! He spit all over me. Oh my God!
(*He wipes himself frantically with the sheet. The* Boy *smiles at the audience. Salem works her way under the sheets to the head of the bed and pokes her head out.*)

SALEM/   What's going on?

KENT/   Oh, I can't stand it. The little prick! Oh God! I'll have to take a shower! Aaah! Oh my God! What a rotten thing to do!

(*He rushes to the stage right door and goes inside, slamming the door behind him.* Salem *speaks to the* Boy *from the bed. The* Boy *does not turn to her but continues making faces to the audience.* Kent *can be heard groaning behind the door.*)

SALEM/ When I was about ten I think, little boy, I'd just returned home from a car trip to the county fair with my family. My father, my mother, my sisters and brothers. We'd just gotten home after driving for about two hours, and it had just gotten dark, but none of us had spoken for the whole trip. Are you listening. It was the same as though we'd all been asleep, and we drove in the driveway, and my father stopped the car. But instead of any of us getting out right away like we usually did we all just sat in the car staring ahead and not speaking for a very long time. I was the first to get out and start walking toward the cement steps that led to the porch and I could hear my family behind me. My father, my mother, my sisters and brothers. And I could hear all four doors of the car slam one after the other like gun shots from a rifle. And I could hear their feet following me up the stairs to the porch right behind me. Very silent. I was leading them sort of and I was only about ten years old. I got to the top of the stairs and I was standing on the porch. I was the first one there and I turned to see them and they all looked right at me. All staggered because of the steps, and all their eyes staring right at me. I saw them like that just for a second, and then do you know what I did little boy? I spit on the very top step just before my father stepped down. And just as he stepped on that little spot of spit that had nothing dirtier in it than cotton candy and caramel apple, my whole family burst into noise like you never ever heard. And my father took off his belt that he'd just bought at the county fair. A black leather belt with a silver buckle and a picture of Trigger engraved on the front. And my father took one more step to the top of the porch with the belt hanging down from his right hand and the buckle clinking on the cement. Then he swung his arm around slowly behind his back so that the belt dragged through the air following his wrist and came back so fast that all I could hear was a crack as it hit my ankles and knees and I fell. Then they were silent again and waited there on the steps until my father put the belt back through the loops and buckled the buckle and hitched his jeans up over his hips. Then they all went into the house in a line. My father first, my mother second, my sisters and brothers third. And I stayed there in a ball, all rolled up, with my knees next to my chin and my hands rubbing my ankles. And I felt very good that they'd left me there by myself.

(*The telephone rings; the* Boy *picks up the receiver and answers.*)

BOY/ Hello. What? How did you know where I was.

SALEM/ Who is it?

KENT/ (*From behind the door, yelling*) Salem! I do have diarrhea after all!

BOY/ (*To the telephone*) If I told you it wouldn't make any difference. What difference? I'm in a hotel somewhere. Why don't you leave me alone.

SALEM/ Your papa?

BOY/ Or else what. You threaten me with what. Warm Coca Cola? Refried beans? Wormy corn? A hammock at night?

SALEM/ Your mama?

BOY/ I have air conditioning and two Rolls Royces. Match that, baby.

SALEM/ Your sisters and brothers?

KENT/ Salem!

BOY/ Later, man. Tell it to the old lady. I'm out here on my own. Adios. (*He hangs up the phone and stands; he turns to* Salem.)

SALEM/ Your papa, right? He wants to know where you are?
(*The* Boy *crosses up to the stage right bed and feels the mattress, then takes off his pants and climbs into the bed and gets under the sheets.*)

KENT/ Salem! I won't be able to move!

SALEM/ Now you're in muy mucho trouble, kid.

BOY/ What do you know about trouble, mom?

SALEM/ Mom?

BOY/ You ever had Mexican ranchers ride into your village at two in the morning and kill your father and steal your sisters and brothers for working in the fields for twelve hours a day for a bowl of soup. Lord have mercy.

SALEM/ That sounds like a movie.

BOY/ I was in a movie once.

SALEM/ Yeah?

BOY/ I had to follow this cat around with a palm fan while he scored on all the native chicks.

SALEM/ Did he ride a horse?

BOY/ How do you score chicks on a horse?

SALEM/ Well he could get off now and then.

BOY/ You mean he rides from village to village and leaves the broads pregnant, and then the doctor comes around and asks them who the man was, and they all say: "I don't know. He never told me his name," and then you hear this, "Hi Yo Silver! Away!" in the distance?

SALEM/ Maybe.

BOY/ No, this guy was very cool. He wore linen shirts and hand made Campeche boots and one of those straight brimmed Panamanian hats and a pistol with abalone plates on the handle. And nobody bugged him because they never knew what he was really like, you dig? Like a jaguar or an ocelot. They look very together and calm. Like you could walk up to one and just pet him gently on the nose and feel his silky fur, but you don't do that because they have something else going on that you're not sure about. Something hidden somewhere. Well this cat was like that and even moved like a jaguar. You know, sort of slinky. He hardly ever talked, and when he did it was like a rumble, like a purr.

KENT/ (*Still behind the door*) Salem! It's getting worse! It's very, very loose!

SALEM/ So what did he do?

BOY/ Who?

SALEM/ The guy with the linen shirts.

BOY/ That's what I'm saying. He didn't have to *do* anything. He just sat around and did his stick and everything was taken care of. No worry about a place to sack out. No worry about food or booze. And when he felt like splitting he just took off. But the movie was a drag because they forced him to blow his cool at the end.

SALEM/ How?

BOY/ What difference. They just did. In real life he never would. I mean a cat like that doesn't get all turned around when some villager make a wise crack about his hat.

SALEM/ That's what happened?

BOY/ Yeah. This fool walked up and told him his hat made him look like a clown or something like that and the cat fell right into a trap where the villagers tore him up and ate him alive. Like cannibalism or something.

SALEM/ Then what happened?

BOY/ All the women committed suicide.

SALEM/ Really?

BOY/ Yeah. But that's what I want to be like, mom. Except I wouldn't blow my cool. Not about a hat anyway. A hat's just something you wear to keep off the sun. One hat's as good as another. You blow your cool about other shit. Like when a man spits in your face.
(Kent *enters from the stage right door dressed in a straight brimmed Panamanian hat, a linen shirt, hand made boots, underwear, and a pistol around his waist. His skin is now pale white and should appear made up. He crosses center stage, strutting.*)

KENT/ Well! I feel like a new man after all that. I think I finally flushed that old amoeba right down the old drain.
(*He struts up and down, hitching his pistol on his hips.*)

BOY/ Ole!

KENT/ Yes, sir! Nothing like a little amoebic dysentery to build up a man's immunity to his environment. That's the trouble with the States you know. Everything's so clean and pure and immaculate up there that a man doesn't even have a chance to build up his own immunity. They're breeding a bunch of lily livered weaklings up there simply by not having a little dirty water around to toughen people up. Before you know it them people ain't going to be able to travel nowhere outside their own country on account of their low resistance. An isolated land of purification. That's what I'd call it. Now they got some minds, I'll grant you that. But the mind ain't nothing without the old body tagging along behind to follow things through. And the old body ain't nothing without a little amoeba.

SALEM/ Bravo!
(Salem *and* Boy *hum,* "When Johnny Comes Marching Home," *as* Kent *struts more proudly up and down and takes out the pistol and starts twirling it on his trigger finger.*)

KENT/ Yes sir! That's always been true as long as man's been around on this earth and it ain't going to stop just on account of a few high falootin' ideas about comfort and leisure. No sirree! Why it'll get so bad up there that even foreigners won't be able to come in on account of they won't be able to take the cleanliness. Their systems will act the same way in reverse. Nobody can come in and nobody can get out. An isolated land. That's what I call it.

BOY/ Bravo! Bravo!
(Kent *gets more carried away with himself as they hum louder in the background.*)

KENT/ Then the next step is in-breeding in a culture like that where there's no one coming in and no one getting out. Incest! Yes sirree! The land will fall apart. Just take your Indians for example. Look what's happened to them through incest. Smaller and smaller! Shorter life span! Rotten teeth! Low resistance! The population shrinks. The people die away. Extinction! Destruction! Rot and ruin! I see it all now clearly before me! The Greatest Society on its way down hill.

(Salem *and* Boy *stop humming.* Kent *blows imaginary smoke out of the pistol and puts it back in the holster, he sees the* Boy *in his bed and screams.*)

KENT/ What's he doing in my bed!
(*He faints on the floor.* Salem *screams and jumps out of bed, she rushes to* Kent *and feels his wrists and slaps his face, she rushes to the telephone downstage and dials. The* Boy *just sits in bed watching.*)

SALEM/ He's fainted! He's completely out! All because of your dirty water. Is there a doctor in this town?

BOY/ I don't know. Isn't that what the big daddy bear said when he saw Goldilocks? What's he doing in my bed, mothafucka?

SALEM/ (*On the phone*) Hello. Can you get me a doctor right away? Oh shit. Puede un doctor quiere muy- muy- (*To the* Boy) Can you tell him? Please. Tell him I need a doctor. Tell him it's dysentery. Please. I don't speak very well.

BOY/ Pardone me no habla español.

SALEM/ Thanks son. Hello. Puede quiere un doctor de medecina muy pronto aqui! Comprende! No, no, no. Un doctor de medecina. Si! Pronto por favor. Muchas gracias. No, no! Mi esposo es muy enfermo para la turista. Sabe? Bueno. Muchas gracias.
(*She hangs up the phone and rushes back to* Kent, *she slaps his face again and feels his wrists.*)

BOY/   (*Still sitting in bed*) They say the white of an egg is good for poisoning.

SALEM/   Just shut up. He's got the trots.

BOY/   You force about half a dozen egg whites down the throat and then they vomit up the poison. It's very easy. They use it on dogs even.

SALEM/   Look sonny, you just sit tight and don't say another word, or I'll call the chief of police and have them take you back to your mommy and daddy. What he needs is a wet towel. A cold wet towel.
(*She crosses to the stage right door and goes inside, closing the door behind her.*)

BOY/   A wet towel is working from the outside in! With poison you have to work from the inside out!

SALEM/   (*Behind the door*) It's not poison!
(*A loud knock on the stage left door*)

SALEM/   (*Behind the door*) That must be the doctor! Would you answer it please! I'll pay you for it!

BOY/   I don't have any pants on!

SALEM/   (*Behind the door*) Well put them on for Christ's sake!

BOY/   Yes, mam. 'Scuse me, mam.
(*He jumps out of bed and puts his pants back on, another loud knock at the stage left door.*)
Be right with you boss. Just as fast as I can. Yes sir. Just hold tight for Jesus sake. We got a busy house here what with the master sick and all.

SALEM/ Hurry up!

BOY/ Yes, mam. Right away, mam.
(*He goes to the stage left door and opens it. There are a witchdoctor and his son standing in the door; they are both very dark skinned. The* Son *looks exactly like the* Boy *and is dressed the same way. The* Witchdoctor *is dressed in sandals, short black pants, a bright red shirt, a short black jacket with elaborate floral designs on the sleeves and the back, a purple bandana wrapped around his head like a turban with tassels hanging down the back. He has two live chickens tied by the feet and hanging upside down from each of his wrists; he carries a long rope whip in one hand, a long machete hangs from his belt. The* Son *carries a burlap bag full of incense, firecrackers, and candles in one hand, and in the other is a large coffee can full of burning incense, strung with a long leather thong; he swings the can back and forth by the thong so that the smoke from the incense rises. They cross center stage. At all times they should behave as though they have nothing to do with the play and just happen to be there.*)

BOY/ The doctor is here, mam! Shall I show him in?

SALEM/ (*Behind the door*) Show him where Kent is and tell him I'll be right there!

BOY/ (*Motioning to* Kent) Doctor, this is Kent. Kent is very sick from poisoning and needs your help.

DOCTOR/ (*Crouching down next to* Kent) Pason!

BOY/ Si.

SON/ Pason!

DOCTOR/ Pason! Aeey!

BOY/ Si.
(*The* Witchdoctor *rises slowly and motions to his* Son *to set down the bag and the incense can, then he motions to the two suitcases on the floor. The* Son *goes to each suitcase and carries them over to* Kent, *who remains limp on the floor through all this. The* Son *then opens each suitcase and dumps the contents all over* Kent; *these should be money and various tourist items. The* Witchdoctor, *at the same time, crosses center stage and sets the chickens on the floor; he then picks up the incense can and waves it several times over the chickens, crossing himself as he does this; he crosses to* Kent *and does the same thing with him and then whips* Kent *across the back several times with the rope. He goes through the same actions over and over again, crossing from the chickens to* Kent, *and then back to the chickens, while the* Son *takes out incense from the burlap bag and places it in small metal bowls, also from the bag, in a circle all around* Kent. *Then he lights each bowl of incense very methodically and crosses himself as he does this; then he goes to the bag again and takes out candles; he places the candles also in a circle around* Kent *and lights each one as he did with the incense; after this is finished he goes to the bag and takes out a string of firecrackers and lights it at* Kent's *feet. All during this, they chant these words over and over in any order*

they want to: "Quetzal, Totzal, Cobal, Pason."
They can repeat each word several times or
say them in series; the whole thing should be
very habitual and appear as though they'd done
it a thousand times before. They should now
and then look at the audience and wonder why
it's there, as they go through the motions.
Meanwhile, the Boy *crosses to the downstage*
apron and talks directly to the audience, as a
tourist quide speaking to tourists. He crosses
casually back and forth. Salem *remains behind*
the stage right door.)

BOY/ The people in this area speak the purest Mayan
existing today. The language has changed only
slightly since the days of the great Mayan civil-
ization before the time of the conquest. It's
even more pure than the Mayan spoken by the
primitive Lacandones, who live in the state of
Chiapas. It's even purer by far than the Mayan
spoken in the Yucatan, where much Spanish
and Ladino admixtures have been added. In
short, it's very pure and nearly impossible for
an outsider to learn, although many have tried.

SALEM/ (*Still behind the door*) Tell him to do whatever
he has to! Don't worry about the money!

BOY/ The man here is the most respected of all, or I
should say, his profession is. But then, we can't
separate a man from his profession, can we?
Anyway, there are several witchdoctors for
each tribe and they become this through inher-
itance only. In other words, no one is elected to
be a witchdoctor. This would be impossible
since there is so very much to learn and the only
way to learn it is to be around a witchdoctor all

the time. Therefore the witchdoctor's oldest son, whom you see here, will fall heir to his father's position. He listens carefully and watches closely to everything his father does and even helps out in part of the ceremony as you see here. A great kid.

SALEM/ Tell him that I'm sick too and may need some help!

BOY/ The people of the village are very superstitious and still believe in spirits possessing the body. They believe that in some way the evil spirits must be driven from the body in order for the body to become well again. This is why you see the witchdoctor beating the man. This is to drive the evil spirits out. The firecrackers are to scare them away. The incense smoke, or copal, as it's called here, is to send the prayers up to the god. They believe the smoke will carry the prayers to heaven. The candles are so that the god will look down and see the light and know that there's somebody praying down here, since the god only looks when something attracts his attention.

SALEM/ I think I've got the same thing?

BOY/ Although there are several European doctors in town, the people will not go to them for help. Instead they call for the witchdoctor who comes to their home and prays for them and beats them up and then goes to the top of the mountain where the god of health is supposed to be. There is an idol there that the witchdoctor prays to in much the same way as you see here. Please don't try to go to the top of the mountain alone though, without a guide, because it can be very dangerous. Last year a group of students from an American university went up there and tried to steal the idol for an anthropological study and they were almost killed. It's perfectly safe with a guide though, and you can always find me in front of the pharmacy. Or just ask someone for Sebastian Smith.

SALEM/ It's getting worse now! It's very, very loose!

BOY/ Of course, in the days before Christ, they used to sacrifice young girls to the gods. But now that's been made illegal by the government so the people use chickens instead. That's what the two chickens are for. They usually give the poor chicken a little drink of cane liquor to deaden the pain but sometimes they don't even bother. You'll notice a slight mixture of Catholic ritual incorporated into the pagan rites. This has become more and more apparent within the last century but the people still hold firmly to their primitive beliefs.

SALEM/ Ask him if he can come in here as soon as he's done with Kent!

BOY/ The marriage is fixed by the family, and the partners have nothing to say in this matter. The girls begin having babies at the age of fourteen and usually have about fifteen children before they die. The average life expectancy is thirty-eight for women and forty-two for men. The women hold equal property rights as the men and get paid a salary by the men for each baby they have. The eldest son in each family always falls heir to the father's property. The puberty rites for boys are very stringent here and vary all the way from having the thumbnail on the right hand peeled away to having three small incisions made with a razor on the end of the penis. By the time the penis has healed they believe the boy has become a man.

SALEM/ Tell him to hurry! It's getting much worse!
(*At this time, the* Son *takes all of* Kent's *clothes off except his underwear, and piles them neatly at his feet, while the* Witchdoctor *takes out his machete and waves it over the chicken. He also swings the coffee can back and forth and chants more intensely.*)

BOY/ At this time the clothes are removed from the man in preparation for the sacrifice. The chickens will be decapitated and their bodies held over the man to allow the blood to drop onto his back. This will allow the good spirits to enter his body and make him well again. The clothes will be burned since it is believed that the evil spirits still reside in his clothes. And if anyone should put them on they would have bad health for the rest of their days and die within two years.

SALEM/ I can't stand it anymore!

BOY/ After this, the witchdoctor will pray over the heads of the chickens and then take them to the top of the mountain, where he will throw them into the fire and then do some more praying. Now is the time for the sacrifice. For those of you who aren't used to this sort of thing you may close your eyes and just listen, or else you could keep in mind that it's not a young girl but a dumb chicken.

(*The* Son *goes to the chickens and stretches their necks out on the floor. The* Witchdoctor *cuts off both their heads with one stroke of his machete.* Salem *screams from the bathroom.*)

SALEM/ Oh my God!
(*The* Witchdoctor *takes both the chicken bodies and holds them over* Kent *so that they bleed on his back. The* Son *chants over the heads and crosses himself; the* Witchdoctor *also chants.* Salem *enters from the bathroom; her skin is pale white now; she clutches her stomach and goes in circles around the stage in great pain.*)

BOY/ Why madame, your sunburn is gone.

SALEM/ I'm sick and pale, and dying from the same thing as Kent. What's happened to Kent? How is my Kent? How is my boy?

BOY/ He's dead.

SALEM/ No he's not dead. I'm not dead and I have the same thing. The same rotten thing.

BOY/ You're both dead.
(*The* Son *and the* Witchdoctor *continue to chant and stay in their positions watching* Salem *and the* Boy, *but remaining uninvolved.* Salem *goes in circles and paces back and forth clutching her stomach.*)

SALEM/ Don't tell me that. I wish I was dead but I'm not. Don't tell me that now when I need comfort and soothing. When I need an alcohol rub down and some hot lemonade. How can you speak to me in this way. I'm having cold chills. My body is burning alive. How will I make it back to my home?

BOY/ Plane or train or bus or car.

SALEM/ Don't tell me that now. Look at me sweat. Who's around who knows what to do? Who is there?

BOY/ The doctor's right here.
(Salem *becomes more and more delirious, clutching her stomach and head.*)

SALEM/ I'm seeing things in front of my eyes. I'm shaking all over. Look at me shaking. What's going on! My eyes are popping out of my head.

BOY/ You could lie down. Kent's lying down.

SALEM/ Kent's faking. Kent's playing dead while I'm the one who needs attention. Look at me now. Just look. Don't look at him.

BOY/ I see.

SALEM/ No you don't. You said I was dead so you must see a corpse. Now I'm getting scared, you know.

BOY/ How come?

SALEM/ You wouldn't understand. Look at me. I'm not even dressed.
(*The* Boy *crosses and picks up off the floor a Mexican poncho that was one of the items in the suitcase and hands it to* Salem, *who keeps pacing up and down.*)

BOY/ You can wear this.

SALEM/ No, no. I need something like a nice wool sweater and some nice cotton slacks and a nice big bracelet and some jade earrings and some nice warm shoes. And I need to have my hair all done and my nails fixed up and someone to take me out to dinner.

BOY/ Well wear this, mom, and as soon as daddy's well, we'll all go out to dinner.

SALEM/ All right. All right. But don't call me names.
(*She puts on the poncho and then continues to pace as the* Boy *crosses to* Kent *and feels his head. The* Witchdoctor *and his* Son *continue to chant.*)

SALEM/ I feel so silly.

BOY/ Don't feel silly. They keep you very warm. It's what the natives wear.

SALEM/ Not about that. I feel silly because I'm sick and cold, and Kent's very sick, and I'm not sure at all about what I should do, about who I should ask about what I should do. I don't speak and I'm not from here.

BOY/ Ask me. I've been around.

SALEM/ Around where, for instance? Around what? You've got built-in immunity. Just look at me. I'm almost naked.
(*The* Boy *begins to put on each item of* Kent's *costume as they continue.*)

BOY/ Better than being too weighted down with extra junk you don't need. Just take a canteen, some sandwiches.

SALEM/ Take them where? I'm staying here. You're the

one who's got to leave. We rented this room, Kent and me. *We're* on vacation, *you're* not.

BOY/ Good. I hope you have a nice trip back.

SALEM/ Not back! Here! We've just come here! We're not going back now! You can see Kent lying there dead and at the same time tell me I should have a nice trip back? I can tell you it won't be so nice!

BOY/ Well, I hope you have a nice time here then.

SALEM/ Put down those clothes! Get out of this room before I call the police.

BOY/ Someone pulled out the phone.

SALEM/ I don't care! I want you to leave.

BOY/ You'll need me around to translate. To run downstairs to the pharmacy and get what you need.

SALEM/ What will I need?

BOY/ Well, you'll need sterile white gauze and tubes of green ointment and different kinds of hot and cold salve. And you'll need ice packs and pain killers and iodine and stimulants and penicillin pills.

SALEM/ I haven't been gored by a bull. I've been screwed by amoeba and I don't even know what they look like. They probably have little white heads and red eyes and two legs, but I know they don't go on forever.

BOY/ They'll follow you around wherever you go.

SALEM/   Don't try to scare me, sonny. I've been around. You don't know the first thing about amoeba. You could eat chile right off the street and not catch a thing. It's me who's in danger, not you. So don't give me advice. Look how strong you are. Just look. Now look at me.

BOY/   Well, how do I look?

SALEM/   Come up here boy and stand straight. Come on up here! Come on! Come on! Come up here with me and let's see what you look like now that you've grown.
(*The* Boy *crosses up to her, now fully dressed in* Kent's *costume.* Salem *takes him by the hand and leads him downstage center; she leads him back and forth by the hand downstage and speaks to the audience as though it were a market place full of villagers. The chanting gets louder in the background.*)
Mira! Mira! Mira! Look what is here! Look what I have for you! For any of you who has the right price! Quantos pesos por el niño! El niño es muy bravo no! Si! He has come to me from the hills with his father's clothes and his mother's eyes! Look at his hands! How strong! How brave! His father says he is old enough now to work for himself! To work for one of you! To work hard and long! His father has given him over to me for the price of six hogs! I give him to you now for the price of twelve! Doce paygar por el niño aqui! Come on! Come on! No?
(*She drags the* Boy *by the hand, down off the edge of the stage into the audience, and walks up and down the aisles showing the* Boy *to the people and yelling loudly. The* Witchdoctor *and his* Son *watch* Salem *and the* Boy *in the same*

*way the audience does, and in some way re-
flect the audience's reaction back to them, but
go on with their chanting.* Kent *remains limp.*)
Quantos pesos por el niño! Quantos! Quantos!
What more could you want? At this time in his
life, he is worth more to you than all the
ponchos you could make in three months. In
four months! He'll bring in your sheep at night!
He'll take them out in the morning! He'll scare
away dogs and crows and cut up your corn!
Feel his calves and thighs! Look at his eyes
and his mouth! He's honest too! He'll never
steal or lie or cheat! He also sings songs from
his native tribe and carves wooden animals in
his spare time! He'll speak to you only when
he's spoken to and he'll never ever laugh behind your back! He's trained to haul wood and
carry water up to thirty miles without resting
once! What more could you want? What more
could you ask? You can always re-sell him,
you know. And you'll never get less than six
hogs! His skin is clean! He has no scars! Probably cleaner skin than any of yours! His hair is
free of lice and ticks! He has all his teeth! What
are you waiting for? How much will you pay?
Cuantos! Cuantos! You'll never get another
chance! How much will you pay for this boy?
(*The phone suddenly begins to ring.* Salem *and
the* Boy *stop immediately and turn to the stage;
they are in the center aisle at the back of the
theater. The* Son *and the* Witchdoctor *stop
chanting and just stare at the phone as it rings;
the* Son *slowly crosses up to the phone and answers it.*)

SON/   Hello. What? (*He holds one hand over the receiver and yells to the* Boy.) It's for you! (*The*

Boy *crosses down the aisle toward the phone.*
Salem *remains where she is.*)

SALEM/   Tell them you're going away on a trip. Tell them
you're going to the U.S.A.! Tell them whatever
they want to hear!
(*The* Boy *takes the phone from the* Son *and
answers it. The* Son *goes back to the* Witchdoctor *and they both begin chanting quietly
over* Kent's *body again. The lights slowly begin
to fade at this point; also the fan begins to die
down.*)

BOY/   (*On the phone*) Bueno. Si. Si. Esta bien. No. Si.
Volver a la casa. Si. Si. En esta noche. No. No
me gusto. Si. Esta bien. No. Esta mejor.

SALEM/   What do they want! Tell them you're going with
me!
(*She begins to slowly cross down the aisle
toward the stage now.*)

BOY/   Estoy muy triste aqui. Si. Bueno. Tu Tambien?
Bueno. Hasta luego. Si. Buena noche papa.
Adios.
(*He hangs up the phone and stares at* Salem,
*who crosses slowly toward him up the aisle.
The* Witchdoctor *and his* Son *just stand staring
at* Kent *and chanting softly. The lights keep fad-
ing.* Kent *remains on the floor.*)

BOY/   That's my father.

SALEM/   You father is dead. You're going with me. We
have more things to do.

BOY/   That's the first time he ever speaks on a phone
in his life. He says to start walking down the

road toward my home and he'll start walking toward me, and we'll meet half way and embrace.

SALEM/ How will you meet in the dark? You can't even see the road.

BOY/ We'll meet in the light. My home is far from here. We'll meet as the sun come up. We'll see each other from very far off and we'll look to each other like dwarfs. He'll see me, and I'll see him, and we'll get bigger and bigger as we approach.

SALEM/ You and your father will die in your hut. You could come with me. I could teach you how to drive a car. We could go everywhere together.

BOY/ Then we'll tell about where we've been, and I'll sing songs that he's never heard.

SALEM/ Your father is deaf!
(*She gets closer to the* Boy *as the lights get dimmer.*)

BOY/ And we'll sit together and smoke by the side of the road, until a truck come by heading toward my home. And my father will kiss me good-bye and climb on the back and drive off, and I'll wait for another truck going the other way. A pale blue truck with a canvas back, carrying chickens and goats, and a small picture of the Madonna on the dashboard, and green plastic flowers hanging from the rear view mirror, and golden tassels and fringe around the window, and striped tape wrapped around the gear shift and the steering wheel, and a drunk driver with

a long black beard, and the radio turned up as
loud as it goes and singing Spanish as we drive
out into the Gulf of Mexico and float to the other
side.

SALEM/ You'll never make it alive!
(*The lights dim out and the fan stops as* Salem
reaches the Boy.)

LA TURISTA
ACT TWO

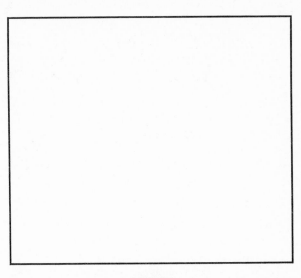

SCENE

The set is organized exactly the same as Act I except the impression this time is that of an American hotel room. All the color is gone from Act I and replaced by different shades of shiny tan and gray. The signs on each door are in English and read "BATHROOM" and "PLEASE DO NOT DISTURB" in black and white. The telephone is plastic. The fan is gone. The suitcases at the foot of each bed are matching plastic. Kent *is in the stage right bed propped up by pillows and sleeping with a thermometer hanging out his mouth. He wears long underwear.* Salem *is in the bathroom. She wears American plastic clothes. The lights come up fast. Loud knocks on the stage left door.* Kent *remains asleep.* Salem *comes out of the bathroom and crosses to the door. She opens it and* Doc, *played by the actor who played* Witchdoctor, *is standing in the doorway with his son,* Sonny, *played by the actor who played* Boy. Doc *is dressed like a country doctor from Civil War times, with boots, a coat with tails, string tie, suspenders, a pistol carried in a shoulder holster, wide brimmed black hat, and a large black satchel with supplies.* Sonny *is dressed exactly the same as* Doc *but without the satchel and pistol.*

SALEM/ Oh good. Finally. Come in. You *are* the ones from the clinic?
(*They both enter.*)

DOC/ Yes, mam. (*Takes off his hat.* Sonny *follows suit.*)

SALEM/ You brought help? You didn't have to bring help. It's nothing serious.

DOC/ No, mam. This here's my boy, Sonny.

SALEM/ How do you do?

SONNY/ All right.

DOC/ He's tagging along. Learning the trade. Apprenticeship, you know.

SALEM/ Well there he is.

DOC/ Let's have a look.
(*He crosses to* Kent *and sits beside him, checking his eyes, forehead, etc., as he talks.* Kent *appears to sleep through this.* Sonny *and* Salem *stand by.*)

SALEM/ I don't know what to tell you more than what I told you over the phone.

DOC/ Well you ain't told me nothing. Was my secretary or something you must a' spoke to. You ain't told me.

SALEM/ Oh.

DOC/ So tell me somethin'.

SALEM/ Well. You mean symptoms?

DOC/ Somethin'. Gotta go on somethin' when you're treatin' illness. Otherwise you might as well be treatin' health.

SALEM/ Well. He goes in cycles.

DOC/ Cycles?

SALEM/ Yes. One thing and then another.
(*Through this,* Doc *motions to* Sonny *to open up his satchel and hand him different instruments for checking the heart, eyes, ears, mouth, etc. Doc goes through these procedures, while* Salem *paces around.*)

DOC/ From what to what?

SALEM/ From sleep to being awake.

DOC/ Me too.

SONNY/ Same here.

SALEM/ No. No. Not like him. It's not the same. We're talking about something. We'll be talking back and forth and we'll be not necessarily deeply involved in what we're saying, but nevertheless talking. And he'll gradually begin to go away.

DOC/ How do you mean?

SALEM/ You'll see a person. Like you're seeing me now, and I'm talking to you, and you're talking to me, and gradually something happens to me while we're talking, until I disappear.

DOC/ He leaves the room?

SALEM/ No, he falls asleep. Like now. He's sleeping. But before you came, he was talking to me. Now he's asleep.

DOC/ Now look here, mam. I need things like runny nose, aching back, itchy skin, bloody urine, runny bowels. Things like that.

SALEM/ They aren't there. What's there is what you see. Sleeping. I thought it was just fatigue, so we came here to rest and get strong. But it's worse than that. I can tell.

DOC/ How?

SALEM/ By the way you look.

SONNY/ (*Spoken in one breath*) You shouldn't worry, mam. Pa looks like that always when he's checking to see what's wrong. Honest. All the time. And I should know, since I'm always around when he's checking to see what's wrong, and you're not always around. In fact this is the first time ever you've been able to see Pa in action. So you should trust me and him and not yourself.

SALEM/ I know doctors. I've been around doctors and they change faces. They have different faces that tell you what's what. And I can tell what's what from the face he has on. So don't tell me.

DOC/   You'll have to tell me somethin' more, mam, to speed things up.

SONNY/   The more we know the faster we can get to work.

SALEM/   What do you mean? Do you help? You're not a doctor.

DOC/   Look lady, no more dilly dally.

SALEM/   I'm trying to concentrate.

SONNY/   Don't try. You can't concentrate if you try.

SALEM/   Boy! You should be a doctor, Sonny. You have all this valuable information up your sleeve.

SONNY/   I do my best.

DOC/   Symptoms, mam, symptoms.

SALEM/   Symptoms!

SONNY/   Things that show on the outside what the inside might be up to.

SALEM/   I know, I know. Yawning. A lot of yawning, and then a lot of talking, then more yawning and talking, and finally sleep, and then waking and talking and yawning and sleep again. Over and over.
(Doc *stands abruptly*.)

DOC/   I have it! Of Course!

SALEM/   What?

DOC/   We must wake him up immediately. Right now, before it's too late. Help me.

(*He and* Sonny *pull* Kent *out of bed and stand him up.* Kent *remains asleep.*)

SALEM/ What is it?

DOC/ Your husband, mam, is subject to what we call chronic Encephalitis Lethargica, also known as sleepy sickness and as Epidemic Encephalitis, von Economo's Disease. A disease that appears from time to time, especially in spring, in the form of epidemics.

SONNY/ See there. I told ya'.
(Sonny *and* Doc *slap* Kent's *face and begin pacing him around the room as they talk to* Salem. Kent *slowly comes out of sleep into a groggy stupor.* Doc *crosses to his satchel and leaves* Sonny *pacing with* Kent. *He pulls out a medical chart from his satchel and unrolls it; the chart is a nude photograph of* Kent, *with labels and diagrams illustrating encephalitis. He hangs it on the upstage wall as he continues to talk. He points to different sections of the chart with a marker as he gives the speech, like an aging college professor who can't remember his lecture.*)

DOC/ It is a virus infection, attacking chiefly the basal ganglia, the cerebrum, and the brain stem. These undergo dropsical swelling, hemorrhages, and, ultimately, destruction of areas of tissue involving both nerve-cells and fibres. The process may involve other parts of the brain, the spinal cord, and even other organs.

SALEM/ Oh no.

DOC/ The illness begins, usually, with rise of temperature and increasing drowsiness or lethargy, which may gradually proceed to a state of complete unconsciousness. In some cases, however, the patient, instead of being drowsy, passes at first through a stage of restlessness, which may amount to maniacal excitement. As a rule, the drowsiness deepens gradually over a period of a week or more, and accompanying it there appear various forms of paralysis, shown by drooping of the eyelids, squint, and weakness of one or both sides of the face. The nerves controlling the muscles of the throat are also sometimes paralyzed, causing changes in the voice and difficulty in swallowing. In some cases the disease affects the spinal cord, producing severe pain in one or more of the limbs, and it is frequently followed by partial paralysis. Signs of inflammation are not infrequently found in other organs, and hemorrhages may be visible beneath the skin and in the muscles, or blood may be vomited up or passed in the stools. The effects last usually for many months; the patient remains easily tired and somnolent, or frequently showing rigidity of muscle, mask-like faces, festinant gait, and rhythmical coarse tremors, resembling the clinical picture of paralysis agitans and known in epidemic encephalitis as Parkinsonism. Other cases show a considerable resemblance in symptoms to chorea, and still others to the disease known as general paralysis; and many cases which result in physical recovery are left with profoundly deteriorated mental powers.

SALEM/ I knew he was sick. What'll we do? We were on our way to Mexico, doctor. To give him a rest.

SONNY/ A rest?

SALEM/ Yes. I mean to get him better.

DOC/ There is no specific treatment for the disease, but he must be kept in motion and, if possible, induced to talk. The more motion the better, lest it prove fatal. Benzedrine sulphate is also useful in some patients at this stage.

SALEM/ Do you have some?

DOC/ Sure do. You take his arm, mam, with Sonny, and walk him up and down while I get the pills. Keep him moving at all cost.
(*She follows his instructions while* Doc *gets a bottle of pills out of his satchel.* Kent *is yawning.*)

SALEM/ What a thing to have. It sounds just terrible. And we were on our way for a vacation.
(*When* Kent *speaks he is in a world unrelated to anything on stage, even when he talks to the other actors and even when his dialogue seems coherent to the action around him.*)

KENT/ Haa! Your hands are something, boy. Fast hands.

SONNY/ He talks.

DOC/ Good, good. Keep him going. Keep him talking.

KENT/ Don't have screwy knuckles like that just playing hand ball or something. Hand ball you use the palm. But bloody knuckles. Wowee.

SALEM/ What?

DOC/ Don't worry. Give him these when you get a chance, but let him talk.

SALEM/ What are they?

DOC/ Benzedrine. Just keep him going.
(*He hands Salem the pills, then crosses to the
stage left bed and takes off his coat and sits on
the bed with his hands clasped behind his head,
and watches. Kent paces, with Sonny and
Salem holding onto his arms.*)

KENT/ Just don't worry. It carries me through.

SALEM/ Shouldn't you be doing something else for him,
doctor? What are you doing now?

SONNY/ You should let Pa alone now, mam. It's up to us
to carry through with what he says.

DOC/ Just keep him movin'.

SALEM/ What are *you* doing?

DOC/ Thought I'd take a snooze here for a bit. It's
been a long ride out.
(*He closes his eyes and begins to sleep, as
Sonny and Salem keep Kent pacing.*)

SALEM/ Great. You're doing nothing.

SONNY/ It *was* quite a ride, mam.

SALEM/ What do I care about your ride. You're *supposed* to ride when you have a sick patient.
Doctors have been riding for years. Back and
forth. Wherever they're needed, they go. They
even have to swear that they'll do it before they
can—

KENT/ How should anyone know. They get thrown into
it.

SALEM/ (*To* Doc) Listen, is he eventually supposed to come out of it, or do we just keep this up forever? Hey!

SONNY/ Shh! He's asleep, mam.

SALEM/ Well how are we going to tell when he's all right?

SONNY/ Pa will give the sign.

SALEM/ But he's asleep.

SONNY/ He wakes up every half hour on the hour, then goes back to sleep.

SALEM/ How come?

SONNY/ He used to raise puppies. They have to be fed once every half hour until they're at least nine weeks old.

KENT/ A doctor shouldn't fall asleep on the job.

SALEM/ That's right. What is he, a veterinarian?

SONNY/ If he's on the job and he's too tired to do the job justice, then he should fall asleep and wake up rested to do a good job.

SALEM/ Do you want some uppies, Kent?

SONNY/ Not yet.
(*They keep pacing with* Kent, *while* Doc *sleeps. The pacing should change back and forth, from* Kent *pulling them along, to them pulling* Kent *along; it should cover the entire stage and continually change speed and quality. At no time do* Sonny *and* Salem *let go of his arms.*)

KENT/ I know that type. That sneaky type. That member of the horror show who disappears into it when he doesn't want to be seen, and then pops out when he does.

SALEM/ I don't know how to talk to him.

SONNY/ Just relax. Let him do the talking.

KENT/ That type came to our door once, with my family inside, where they always were. Watching horror shows on—— The monster's always a nice guy. Notice that. Always nice.

SALEM/ Kent! Wake up.

SONNY/ Shh. Let him go.

SALEM/ But we were going to Mexico.

KENT/ So he knocks on the door, and Pa answers it, and the guy comes in with a brief case. Right into the house. And the house is in the middle of the prairie, with nothing around but prairie and one huge factory where they make something inside that you never see outside. All you can see is smoke coming out. And he comes in, with Ma and brothers and sisters all around chewing on the furniture, and Pa dying for a smoke.
(Doc *yawns, then begins snoring loudly.*)

SALEM/ Doctor! Do something!

KENT/ Shh! And Pa can hardly walk from lack of everything he needs. So the guy from the factory sits down next to Pa, who's dying, and says to him I see you've got all these lovely sons and daughters, and Pa nods. Then the guy from the horror show says and I see they're all dying, and Ma nods. And the guy says I know you never get a chance to see inside our factory, to see what exactly it is that we make, and they shake their heads. So right now I'm going to give you a chance, and he opens up the brief case which is loaded with different packs of cigarettes. Pa smiles and licks his nose. The kids gather around. Ma faints. The guy says I'm going to make you a little offer, my friend.

SONNY/ Pa!

KENT/ If you change each one of the stupid names you gave your eight kids, from whatever it is now, to one of the eight brand names of our cigarettes, I'll set you up in your own little business and give you all the smokes you need. So don't go shoving benzedrine in my face.

SALEM/ It's for your own good, Kent.

SONNY/ Pa! I think we need help.

KENT/ You're doing fine. You don't even have to hold on. The pace is great.

SONNY/ Don't believe him, mam. They all say that. And just at the point when they say that, you know that the last thing in the world you should do is to do what they say.

SALEM/ But maybe he means it. Kent? Are you O.K.?

SONNY/ Just keep hold a' that arm, lady. Do exactly the opposite of whatever he wants. Believe me. I've learned.

KENT/ You're no doctor.

SONNY/ Last week Pa and I were out at the Tuttle farm, out past Lansingville, to see old lady Tuttle, since her neighbors called us up and asked us to go give her a look-see, since she was doing a lot of fiddle playin' late at night and they was all worried. So we rode out there about 3 A.M. one mornin' last week, thinkin' we'd catch her at it if she was really doin' what they said she was doin', and she was all right. She was doin' it.

SALEM/ Look, we have to get him well so we can get started on our trip.

SONNY/ Sittin' out there on her front porch just as plain as day. Tappin' her foot and rockin' to the tune she was doin'. Think it was, "Hang Toad's Got No Stock In My Mind." Somethin' like that.

SALEM/ Doctor!

SONNY/ So we sneak up on her through the shrub pine and sit there in the dark for a spell just listenin' to that fine old fiddle a' Mrs. Tuttle's.
(Doc *wakes up suddenly and sits up on the bed; he stands abruptly and puts on his coat; he checks his watch. The rest keep pacing.*)

DOC/ What!

SONNY/ Just tellin' the lady here about old lady Tuttle, Pa.
(Doc *gets involved in the story and wanders downstage.*)

DOC/ Oh yes. Well it was a strange night. A night the

likes a' which could make you figure old lady Tuttle was the only one in the world to speak of, and we two, my boy and I, we was like shrub pine. Just lookin' on. Growin' slowly. Rooted in one place. Lettin' seasons change us. And Mrs. Tuttle was playin' for us like she was playin' for the world of bushes and plants and insect life.

KENT/ So Pa was set up in business at last.

DOC/ Shut up! Keep him still!
(*They keep pacing* Kent, *while* Doc *comes down and speaks to the audience while walking around.*)

SALEM/ Doctor.

DOC/ So there we was. My boy and I, hidden from view. Invisible to old lady Tuttle. And we noticed after a bit how we was gettin' entranced by that darn fiddle a' hers. That old lady had us hypnotized there for a while, until my boy here realized it and snapped us both out of it.

SALEM/ Doctor! Pay attention to your patient.

DOC/ Well we figured it out between the two of us but only after it was too late. Instead we fell right into her trap and walked right up to her porch just as plain as you please and—

SONNY/ That's not exactly how it went, Pa.

DOC/ You shut up! How it went is no concern of mine or yours. All I want to do is finish up and go home.

KENT/ And leave me stranded.

SALEM/ How can a doctor leave you stranded, Kent?

DOC/ By ridin' out, lady.

SALEM/ I'll call the clinic.

DOC/ Try it!

SONNY/ Pa cut the wires on the way in, mam.

SALEM/ You what! That's rotten.

DOC/ (*To audience*) So we walk right up to old lady Tuttle, who doesn't even see us. Like we're not there, even.

KENT/ That means that I'll fall asleep and never wake up.

SALEM/ Don't be silly. We'll keep you going all night if we have to.

KENT/ What about tomorrow?

SALEM/ And tomorrow we'll go to Mexico.

DOC/ And the closer we get the better we see that she could be anywhere. She couldn't care less.

KENT/ Let go of me. I want to check the phone.

DOC/ Don't let him go at any cost!

KENT/ I want to check on the phone!
(*They keep* Kent *pacing.*)

DOC/ (*To audience*) There's one thing I could never stand in all those years ridin' back and forth treatin' sores and wounds and shrunken hands.

SONNY/ What's that, Pa?

DOC/ That's the absolute unwillingness that all them sickly, misfit imbeciles had for going along with what I'd prescribe. You say one thing and they do the exact opposite right off the bat. Soon as you turn your back off they'd go in the wrong direction. Straight into what I was tryin' to lead them out of.

SALEM/ Doctor! He seems to be all right now.

SONNY/ Ya' gotta watch the tricks, mam. Ya' gotta develop an eye for the tricks so you can tell one kind from another kind.

DOC/ It got to a point there, in my traipsin' around, where I felt like a doctor was the last thing needed. Just let the fools work it out for themselves.

SALEM/ He's moving and everything. He's talking and walking. That's what you wanted. Can't we let him go now? Doctor.

DOC/ Sure! Sure enough! Let him go!
(*They all stop still.*)

SALEM/ Kent?
(*They let go of* Kent's *arms and back away.* Kent *remains standing still.* Doc *crosses up to him and checks his eyelids, then steps back.*)

DOC/ All right.

SALEM/ What? He's all right now, isn't he?

DOC/ Sure. Fit as a fiddle.
(Kent *rushes to the phone and picks it up; he*

tries to dial with no success; he freezes as he hangs up the phone.)

KENT/ They cut the wires. The juice.

SALEM/ Kent. We can take off tomorrow if you want.

SONNY/ Why Mexico? Why not Canada, where you'd be less noticeable?

SALEM/ That's right, Kent. In Mexico they're all dark. They'd notice us right off the bat.

DOC/ Especially with a corpse.

SONNY/ They'd notice a corpse anywhere.

SALEM/ What do you mean?

KENT/ Not here. In Lansingville. Get a T.V. in here. Some sandwiches.

SALEM/ No. That's silly. We want to get out, not in.

DOC/ I could stop by once a week.

SALEM/ Here's some pills, Kent. Take some pills. You'll be all right.
(She hands Kent the pills. He holds them in his hand and remains frozen.)
I'll get you a glass of water.
(She exits into the bathroom. Doc and Sonny move in on Kent, who stays frozen.)

SONNY/ Unless ya' want to follow Pa's directions, fool, you'll never get out a' this hole.

DOC/ That's right. Listen to the boy.

SONNY/ He knows what he's sayin', Pa does.

DOC/ Ain't been travelin' through hick town after town, tearin' the scabs off a' infection that otherwise would a' made a corpse out of a live man if the pus wasn't allowed to draw off. Ain't been doin' that and not comin' back with some savvy.

SONNY/ They do it with trees too, so don't feel bad.

DOC/ Just keep yourself movin', son. It's the only way out.
(Salem *enters with a glass of water and hands it to* Kent.)

SALEM/ Here, Kent.

DOC/ See here, your woman's right behind ya', boy.
(Kent *takes the pills and a gulp of water; he hands the glass back to* Salem, *then stands.*)

KENT/ Well. Thanks, Doc. Hope you have a nice trip back.

DOC/ Oh. Well. Nice? Sure. It won't be so nice. I mean it won't be any nicer than it was coming out.

KENT/ How nice was that?

DOC/ So, so.

KENT/ Well I hope it's nicer than that.
(Kent *begins wandering around freely, looking at the walls of the room.*)

SONNY/ That can't be. It's always the same. Dusty, hot. Ya' get tired and rest at the same places along the road, under the same trees.

KENT/ Why's that?

DOC/ Well, that's where the wells are, ya' see. Ya' have to get tired where the water is so's you don't pass 'em by. Otherwise, you're just out a' luck.

KENT/ Don't you carry a canteen or something?

SALEM/ We can take off tomorrow then, Kent. If you feel all right.

KENT/ How will you reserve tickets? The wires are cut. The juice is off.

SONNY/ That's right.

DOC/ Anyway we gotta hang around for a bit to check you out. Make sure ya' don't have a relapse.

KENT/ A what?

DOC/ A relapse. To make sure the same business doesn't start all over again.

SONNY/ You need your bag, Pa?

SALEM/ I could walk down the road and make a call from the pay phone.

DOC/ Ya' see ya' could easily fall back into it if ya' don't watch your step. It depends on a very fragile margin in the basal ganglia. One little jar, and poof. You have to keep the opposite pole in motion in order not to activate the opposite one.

SONNY/ He's right.

SALEM/ Shall I go make reservations, Kent?

DOC/ Not yet! He's in no shape to be wanderin' into the freezin' night the way he is. Out there with the crickets.

KENT/ I think I'll stay.

SALEM/ Well then I'll go.

DOC/ No. You should stay too, lady.

KENT/ Why should she?

DOC/ Well, I mean we'll need somebody to mix up some jasmine tea with honey, and——

KENT/ Sonny can do that.

SONNY/ It needs a woman.

SALEM/ Look. Kent's all right now, so why don't the two of you go back and leave me with him alone.

SONNY/ You're no doctor.

DOC/ Right. Your husband should get some rest now and special tea. Only a doctor with many years experience and——

SALEM/ Just what is your experience?

SONNY/ Don't talk to Pa like that.

SALEM/ And what's this business about cutting wires.

DOC/ We never cut your wires, lady.
(Kent *advances on* Doc *as* Doc *backs up*.)

KENT/ I thought you said before that you cut our wires.

DOC/ Naw. Never did.

KENT/ I was under the impression we were juiceless here. Out of touch. No way of reaching the outside.

DOC/ Try it then. Pick up the phone and try it.

KENT/ Try it, Salem.
(Salem *goes to the phone and picks up the receiver, as* Kent *backs* Doc *around the stage.* Sonny *looks on.*)

DOC/ You could call Berlin if you wanted.

KENT/ Why would we call Berlin if we wanted?

SALEM/ No juice. (*She hangs up.*)

DOC/ Now that's downright silly. Sonny, you give it a try.

KENT/ Don't move Sonny or I'll gun you down. (Sonny *freezes.*)

DOC/ Now go ahead, son. I have a gun. He don't. I'm the one that's armed. Go on now. Let's settle this once and for all.

KENT/ Don't make a move.

DOC/ You got a lot a' gall, bucko. Just 'cause you're feelin' your oats and all, now that you're cured. You're forgettin' pretty fast who got ya' out a' your dilemma. Remember? Your old Doc got ya' out a' what looked to me like suicide. Plain and simple.
(Sonny *stays frozen.*)

SALEM/ Don't say that. Kent, let's just leave.

KENT/ He'll die if he makes a move.

DOC/ Now that's pushin' it right to the edge, mister. You gotta have a full house to be callin' bluffs like that.
(Kent *draws an imaginary pistol and points it at* Doc, *as he moves him around the stage faster.* Sonny *stays frozen.*)

KENT/ It's been proven that the wires are cut. Salem proved it.

DOC/ Now Sonny you just go and give it a check, and then we can leave. Sonny! (*He stays frozen.*)

SALEM/ Kent, let him check the phone if he wants. Then we'll go.

DOC/ Who are you foolin' with a finger. I ain't from Egypt, ya' know.

SALEM/ Look, I'll phone the operator and show you both. (*She moves toward the phone and freezes when* Doc *speaks.*)

DOC/ Don't make a move!
(*He draws his pistol and aims it at* Kent. *Now* Doc *begins backing* Kent *around the stage.* Kent *keeps his finger pointed at* Doc. Salem *and* Sonny *remain frozen in their places.*)

KENT/ Now why in the world—I ask myself why in the world would a doctor from a respectable clinic want to disconnect the phone of a dying man. A man he's supposed to cure. A man who's prepared to pay him two suitcases full of money in exchange for his good health. I ask myself why and come up with only one answer.

DOC/ Now what would that be?

KENT/ That this doctor is up to no good. That this doctor, in cahoots with his fishy son, is planning to perform some strange experiment on this dying man that he don't want to leak out to the outside world. So if this experiment fails no one will be the wiser, and the only one to have lost anything will be the dying man who's dying anyway.
(*They change directions again with* Kent *advancing and* Doc *retreating.*)

DOC/ And I ask myself something too. I ask myself why this dying man who's got nothing to lose but his life accuses the one and only person who could possibly save it of such a silly thing as cutting the wires to his telephone. I ask myself that and come up with only one answer.

KENT/ Yes?

DOC/ That this dying man isn't dying at all. That this here man is aching all over for only one thing. And he cunningly puts the idea into the mind of the doctor, and the doctor then acts it out. The doctor performs the experiment with his faithful son at his side and transforms the dying man into a thing of beauty.

KENT/ How?
(Doc *advances on* Kent.)

DOC/ By beginning slow. From the hair down. Piece by piece. Peeling the scalp away neatly. Carving out the stickiness and placing cool summer breezes inside. In place of the hair goes a grassy field with a few dandelions falling toward the back.

KENT/ And the eyes?

DOC/ Wet spongy moss covers each one and opens into long tunnel caves that go like spirals to the back where the light pours in. The nose swoops down and has crows and chickadees roosting all day on its tip. The doctor's scalpel moves quickly over the mouth.
(Kent *advances on* Doc.)

KENT/ Oh no. The mouth hangs in strips for lips that droop all the way down to the chin. And underneath are thick round teeth with edges sharper than diamonds, so they flash at night when he's eating. The flashes warn everything living within twenty miles, and they stay inside until morning comes.

DOC/ The chin——

KENT/ I told you! You can't see the chin because of the lips. They hang down. And so does the hair. Long sheets of black hair that hang down past its waist and rustle like paper when it runs.
(Doc *advances on* Kent.)

DOC/ Doc and his faithful son stay up through the night thinking of shoulders and arms and a chest for the beast.
(Sonny *makes a sudden move for the phone but freezes when* Kent *yells.*)

KENT/ Hold it! I'll blow you to bits!

DOC/ At 3 A.M., they get down to work. Moving fast and patiently over the torso. The arms dangle down past its hair and gently flow into beautiful womanly hands that look like they've never been outside of goatskin gloves until this very moment.

KENT/ When it jerks up its head and bursts from the leather strap across its thin chest.

DOC/ No! (Kent *advances on* Doc.)

KENT/ But then it's too late. The moment has come for its birth, and nothing can stop it from coming. (Kent *stalks* Doc *with his finger pointed at him; he manipulates* Doc *all over the stage while the others stay frozen in place.*)

DOC/ Not yet! There's the legs and the feet left to do!

KENT/ It opens its arms and its mouth and tests everything out. It feels how the juices drain from its brain, down through the nose and into the mouth where it tastes like honey. He licks. He kicks off the sheets. He rolls off the edge of the stainless steel table that rolls on its tiny rubber wheels straight for the wall.

DOC/ You can't start before——

KENT/ The fall from the table to the floor starts other juices going. He feels the stream of fluid pulling him off the ground and onto his feet.

DOC/ He can't even walk! He doesn't have feet! (Kent *changes his finger from a gun to a knife*

and begins making quick lunges toward Doc,
who jumps back.)

KENT/ He finds the fluid pounds through his legs and
his waist. It catches hold and loosens up. It
draws back and snaps out like a snake. He
moves across the room in two steps and flat-
tens out against the wall. He disappears and
becomes the wall. He reappears on the opposite wall. He clings to the floor and slithers
along. Underneath cages of rats and rabbits
and monkeys and squirrels. He becomes a
mouse and changes into a cobra and then
back on the floor. Then onto the roof.

DOC/ Stop it!
(Doc *fires the pistol.* Kent *keeps advancing; his
gestures and movements become wildly ex-
travagant, like an African dance.* Doc *retreats
to every corner of the room, running away,
while* Salem *and* Sonny *stay frozen.*)

KENT/ Then jumping from roof to roof with his paper
hair flying behind and his lips curling back from
the wind and tasting the juice that's pouring
down from his nose and his ears.
(Doc *fires again.*)
He zigzags sharply around T.V. antennas and
his ears catch the sound of the dogs panting as
they rush up the steps to the top of the roof. He
can hear barking and screaming and whistles.
Beams of white light cut through the night and
follow his trail. Sirens sound through the
streets.
(Doc *fires.*)
He keeps jumping space after space and roof
after roof. And each jump he makes he looks

down right in mid-air between the roof he left behind and the roof he's jumping to. He looks down and he sees a miniature world where things move like bedbugs and ticks. And then he looks up and he sees miniature lights that flick on and off.

(*Kent leaps off the stage and onto the ramp; he runs up the ramp and behind the audience, where he speaks. Doc intercedes with his lines from the stage.*)

DOC/

Now come back down here and stop playin' around!

KENT/

The Doctor is torn by desires that cut through his brain as he leads the hysterical mob on the trail of the beast he once loved.

I ain't playin' around anymore!

Now it must be destroyed. If he could somehow get to the beast ahead of the mob. Trap it somehow in a quiet place between smooth wet boulders, and talk to it calmly.

I'll walk right out on ya', boy!

Perhaps even stroke its long hair and wipe off its chin. To find some way of telling the beast that the mob will calm down if *he* only does.

I'd just a' soon let ya' rot away!

The Doctor makes a dash away from the mob and

DOC/

There ain't nothin' keeping me here.

Now ya' gotta be fair about this!

I done all I could. I diagnosed the disease. I treated what ails ya'! I can't do no more! What more can I do?

I got'ta keep my distance, boy! A doctor has got to keep a distance! I mean I can't go falling asleep on the job!

Look what would happen if that were to happen!

KENT/

ducks into a dark stand of sycamore trees. The mob is confused and frightened without the Doctor. They become enraged and set the forest on fire.

Doc moves away from the flames easily, since he's passed through this section of land many times before on his calls.

He finds a narrow stream, where he usually drinks on his way back and forth, and slowly submerges under the surface. He swims along easily and lets the current propel him downstream. Moving through flowing green plants and yellow goldfish, and surfacing once in a while to check where he is.

The monster has a complete view now, from his perch.

He sees the stream cutting the land in half, with one half on fire, and the other half dark and quiet. He's calmer now and sits on a rock, catching up with his breath.

The Doctor comes up onto the shore panting for breath

DOC/

KENT/

and clutching at long clumps of grass.

He drags himself up on dry land and staggers on through the night. Afraid if he stops for a rest that the beast will be lost forever.

Now the beast begins to even enjoy being up so high. Above everything else but the sky and watching the golden fire move down one side of the stream and consuming everything dark.

(Doc's "look" sequence during this; Doc goes through different gestures that were Kent's in the first Act: running to the bathroom, swaggering, fainting, etc.)

Doc begins to feel lost now in the trees with no living thing around him but leaves that whistle and hum as though sensing the fire's approach. He must find the beast. He begins to think if I were him how would I hide and how would I run? Which way would I go and how would I choose?

I gotta keep strong!

That's my job!

To keep strong and quick and alert!

The beast even likes the idea of not having to move. To sit in one place on a smooth shiny rock and just swivel to different positions and face in different directions.

DOC/

I mean what earthly good would I be to you or to anyone else if I was walkin' around just as sick as my patients? No good at all. Now you can see that as plain as I can. That's why I make a point to keep fit.

That's why I'm always in shape.

Notice that! My eyes are clear! My skin is smooth! My hair is free of lice and ticks! My muscles are well tuned up for any situation! Just watch me! Look at the way I can move if I want! You should trust me, boy! I'll get ya' through! Just let me show ya' the way! You'll have to go with me though! I can't go with you! I'll show ya' how! Step by step. One foot in front of the other foot. Let your arms swing free at the sides. Let the words come.

KENT/

Doc bends slowly downward and finds he moves faster with his head pushing him on. He seeks out the shadowy places, always staying upwind and straining his eyes to find a higher place.

Gently, the monster pulls the moss flaps back from his eyes and lets the wind fill them up.

His beautiful hands stroke the smooth rock.

He chuckles at the spits that the fire makes as it reaches the stream and goes out. Doc's feet slip and clutch the shale rock and sand and his hands grasp for vines and stumps and roots and anything strong enough to hoist his aching body up to the top. The beast stretches and yawns and smiles. He misses only one thing: the face of the Doc the way it used to be, looking down and smiling with his big dark eyes and his scalpel in hand.

(Doc *goes to* Sonny *and* Salem *and shakes them out of their freeze as he continues to talk to* Kent. *Slowly he gets them to move, he points to* Kent *and persuades them to try to bring him back on the stage. They slowly move downstage, like somnambulists. As* Doc *remains on stage talking to* Kent *they move off the stage and onto the ramp toward* Kent. Salem *and* Sonny *hum,* "When Johnny Comes Marching Home Again," *as they close in on* Kent.)

DOC/

Yes sir, ya' won't have no trouble at all if ya' go along with the cure. We'll be unbeatable, the two of us.

I'll get ya' one a' them pinto stallions with a silver saddle and a golden bit.

And hand tooled Indian boots. I'll show ya' how to use a thirty odd six and a forty odd eight. You don't have to worry your head about nothin', boy! We'll walk into each town like they was puddles a' water waiting around for a boot to come by and splash them out a' their hole. We'll always be taken care of, you and me. Always! Just wait and see.

Get him! Grab ahold of his arms! Get him back down

KENT/

Doc almost forgets why he's climbing so fast and so hard until he hears shouts from the dark side of the forest at the base of the hill. They've crossed the river and picked up his trail. Doc pries loose a boulder and lets it crash down the side.

His beautiful hands are bleeding from clawing. His feet feel like they're not even there.

He lunges and pulls toward the top. He twists in and out of small thorny bushes. He squeezes in between cracks in the rock as bullets ring out and torches flare in the sides of his eyes. He uses his mouth to pull himself up, and his diamond teeth blind the mob with their flash. Doc must get there first and escape with the beast.

His arms rip from the shoulders and chest, and juices

DOC/	KENT/
here! Don't let him get away!	gush out down his sides. He must find him there and hide in a cave. His hair tears and floats away, flapping in air like an owl at night looking for mice in the field far below. He must meet him alone for one final time. His teeth drag him up. Dragging the body along. Pulling and chomping down on the earth. Pulling up and chomping down.

(Salem *and* Sonny *make a lunge for* Kent, *who grabs onto a rope and swings over their heads. He lands on the ramp behind* Doc *and runs straight toward the upstage wall of the set and leaps right through it, leaving a cut-out silhouette of his body in the wall. The lights dim out as the other three stare at the wall.)*

THE END